EXCLUSIVE

ELEVATE

TAKE YOUR BUSINESS
TO NEW HEIGHTS

VIKKIMJONES.COM

*Practice daily mindfulness exercises.
*Engage in regular physical activity that you enjoy.
*Prioritize activities that make you feel rejuvenated.
*Set boundaries and say no to commitments that drain your energy or do not align with your priorities.
PRIORITIZE
SELF CARE
GUIDE & WORKBOOK
WRITTEN BY
VIKKI JONES
Walmart
BARNES & NOBLE
BOOKSELLERS
amazon.com
BAM!
BOOKS·A·MILLION

Editor's Note

Dear Readers,

As we find ourselves immersed in the enchanting embrace of this beautiful season, I am thrilled to present to you the latest edition of VMH Magazine. Bursting with vibrant themes that celebrate the journey of reclaiming our authentic identity and embracing courage to conquer trauma, this issue is designed to inspire and uplift your spirits.

In this edition, we explore the transformative power of writing your story for inner freedom and financial benefits. Our expert contributors share their insights and strategies for harnessing the power of storytelling to unlock personal growth and financial success. Discover how the act of writing can not only provide a cathartic release but also open doors to new opportunities and a brighter future.

As we celebrate the beauty of life in this season, it is essential to remember the importance of self-care and self-love. Amidst the hustle and bustle of our daily lives, it is easy to get caught up in celebrating and loving others while forgetting about ourselves.

This edition of VMH Magazine serves as a gentle reminder to always prioritize your own well-being and happiness. Take a moment to pause, reflect, and indulge in the things that bring you joy. Whether it's a rejuvenating spa day, a leisurely stroll in nature, or simply curling up with a good book, remember to carve out time for yourself, for it is in nurturing our own souls that we can truly celebrate and love others.

In addition to our thought-provoking articles, we have curated a collection of editorials and shopping recommendations that are sure to delight. From the latest fashion trends to must-have accessories, we've scoured the market to bring you the most luxurious and coveted items that will add an extra touch of glamour to your life. Indulge in the pleasure of shopping and allow yourself to be inspired by the artistry and craftsmanship that goes into creating these exquisite pieces.

At VMH Magazine, we believe in the power of positivity, celebration, and embracing the beauty that surrounds us. This edition is a testament to that belief, and we hope that the articles and features within these pages will bring a smile to your face and a sense of joy to your heart. May this season be filled with love, laughter, and the courage to conquer any challenges that come your way.

As you immerse yourself in the pages of this magazine, remember to always cherish and nurture yourself. Celebrate your own unique journey and embrace the love and happiness that resides within you. By doing so, you not only enrich your own life but also create a ripple effect of positivity and love that can touch the lives of those around you.

Wishing you a season filled with abundant blessings, cherished moments, and the unwavering belief in your own worth.

Vikki Jones

Editor-in-Chief

CONTENTS

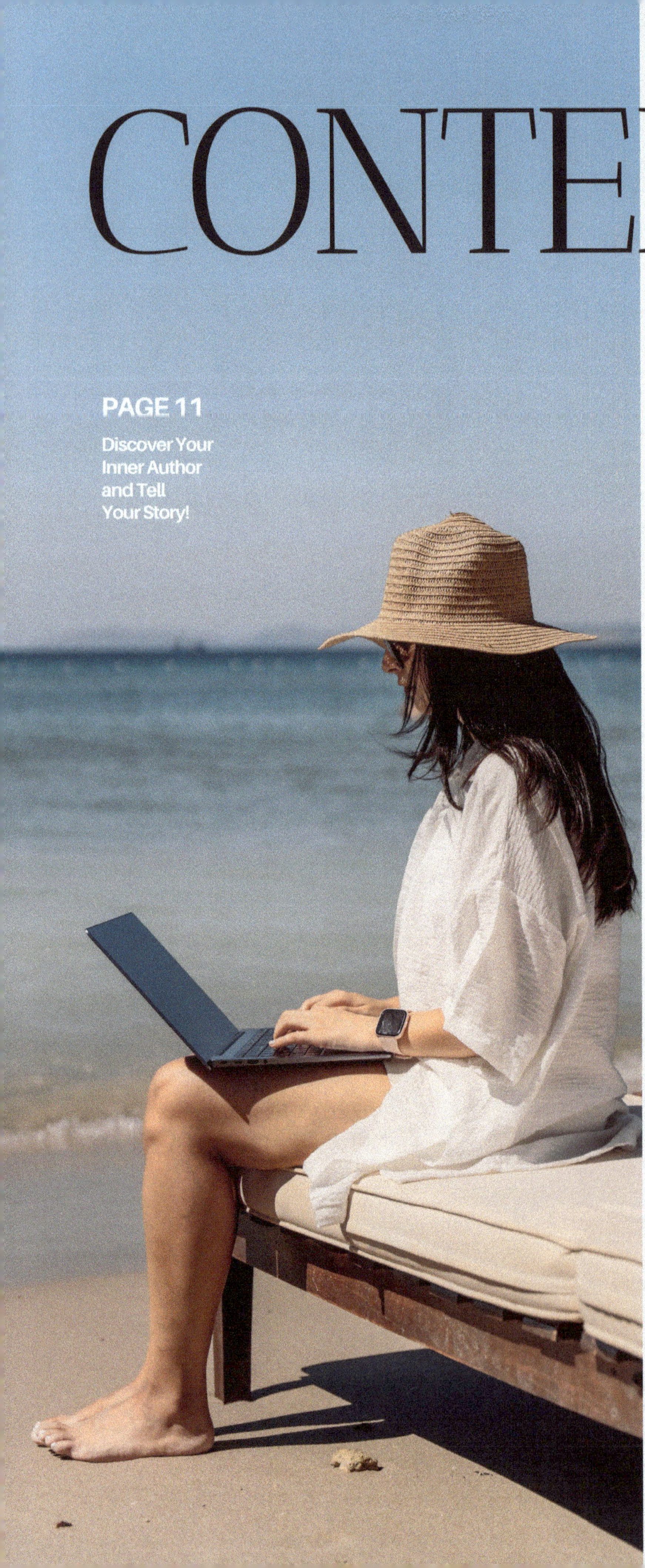

VMH Magazine Created & Designed by Vikki Jones
Cover Image: Vikki Jones
Photography Credit: Vikki Jones

THE HOUSE WITH A BIG HEART

Montreal, Canada

Entre Quatre Murs unveils its design of The House with a Big Heart, located in Town of Mount Royal, in Montreal. Originally built in 1959, the house had not been renovated for several decades and featured typical enclosed rooms and small, narrow, dark hallways. The clients wanted to create a home that would fit their lifestyle. They chose to purchase the property for its location and large garden, but wanted a radical transformation of all its floors so that their young family could thrive within its walls for many years to come.

Photo Credits: Phil Bernard

Photo Credit: Phil Bernard
via VRCOM

ENTRE QUATRE MURS,
UNVEILED THEIR ARCHITECTURAL MASTERPIECE
THE HOUSE WITH THE BIG HEART

WRITTEN BY VIKKI JONES

Montreal's Town of Mount Royal has recently become home to a remarkable architectural gem that is captivating the attention of design enthusiasts. Entre Quatre Murs, a renowned design studio, has unveiled their masterpiece: The House with the Big Heart. Originally constructed in 1959, this house had long been in need of renovation. With its enclosed rooms and narrow, dark hallways, it lacked the openness and functionality desired by its new owners.

The clients, a young family, saw the potential in this property due to its prime location and spacious garden. They sought a radical transformation that would allow them to thrive within these walls for years to come. And Entre Quatre Murs delivered.

To address the lack of natural light, the design team adopted an ingenious approach. They decompartmentalized many of the rooms and created a stunning opening between the first and second floors. As soon as one enters the house, they are greeted by a completely open, white wooden staircase with glass railings that span all three floors. This architectural marvel not only adds an element of lightness but also allows sunlight to permeate throughout the entire house. Additionally, wide openings were made on the rear facade, offering breathtaking views of the garden from every floor.

While the house boasts an open concept layout, careful consideration was given to ensure each room maintains its privacy. Gatline Artis, the owner of the house and designer at Entre Quatre Murs, explains, "We wanted each room to have its privacy, and the views between each space not to detract from the enjoyment of the moment, but simply to allow glimpses of other family members moving from room to room." This design choice provides a sense of calm and privacy within the larger open plan.

The kitchen design takes an unconventional yet captivating approach. Divided into two separate spaces, the front portion consists of three integrated furniture elements that exude lightness and refinement, reminiscent of the living room's bookcases. The absence of wall cabinets emphasizes openness, while delicate legs on the island create a communal table area for family gatherings. Behind the front portion lies an all-black pantry, which creates a striking contrast and discreetly integrates the refrigerator, coffee corner, and small daily appliances. This harmonious combination of aesthetics and functionality perfectly embodies the essence of family life.

On the second floor, private spaces revolve around the central opening of the house. Rather than traditional corridors and partitioned areas, this innovative configuration immerses occupants in the heart of family life as soon as they leave their private spaces. The inclusion of an office as a central piece in the floor plan demonstrates the owners' commitment to their daily work routines. Placed at the center of the space, the large work surfaces act as a central island where the entire family can gather, including the children during homework time.

Even the basement showcases meticulous design choices. Three distinct functions coexist harmoniously without overlapping, thanks to the use of cabinetry modules that visually delineate the gym, pool area, and family room. Custom-made furniture maximizes space utilization while enhancing the functionality of each sub-space. It has truly transformed the basement into a vibrant and multifunctional area enjoyed by the entire family.

Gatline Artis reflects on the journey of creating their dream home: "We were looking for a sweet home, a little cocoon where we could see our children grow up, but above all, we wanted a home that reflected our own image. Creating our own completely bespoke home, in which we could live and thrive for decades to come, was paramount." The process was undoubtedly laborious but immensely rewarding. Each passing season continues to amaze them, exceeding their expectations of functionality and quality of life.

The House with the Big Heart, also known as Dobie, has been recognized with six Gold Certifications at the Grands Prix du Design - 16th edition. It stands as a testament to Entre Quatre Murs' commitment to crafting unique and timeless living spaces. Functionality, materiality, and light serve as the studio's guiding principles, ensuring that their designs enhance the comfort and well-being of their clients.

Beyond design and interior architecture, Entre Quatre Murs believes in creating spaces that evoke deep emotions and truly reflect their clients' identities. Their tight-knit team of talented designers consistently delivers excellence, redefining the concept of "home" on a daily basis.

While the house boasts an open concept layout, careful consideration was given to ensure each room maintains its privacy. Gatline Artis, the owner of the house and designer at Entre Quatre Murs, explains, "We wanted each room to have its privacy, and the views between each space not to detract from the enjoyment of the moment, but simply to allow glimpses of other family members moving from room to room." This design choice provides a sense of calm and privacy within the larger open plan.

Discover Your Inner Author and Tell Your Story!

Your story, your voice, expertly crafted.

1. Personalized Writing Coaching: Our writing coaches will work closely with you, asking a curated list of questions to understand the story you want to tell. With your answers as a guide, we'll help you develop your book, ensuring your personality, voice, and tone shine through.

2. Professional Ghostwriting: Don't have the time or confidence to write your book? Our skilled ghostwriters will transform your ideas and experiences into a captivating manuscript. We'll capture your essence, crafting a book that feels authentically yours.

3. Expert Guidance: Whether you choose writing coaching or ghostwriting, our team will provide expert guidance throughout the process. From outlining and structuring your book to refining the final draft, we'll be there to support you and ensure your vision is realized.

Ready to see your story in print? Visit www.VMHPublishing.net or call 917-409-7420 to learn more about our writing coach and ghostwriting services. Start your journey towards becoming a published author today!

Embrace Your Potential and Achieve Extraordinary Success

Written by Vikki Jones

In a world filled with immense possibilities and endless opportunities, it is disheartening to witness countless individuals holding themselves back from realizing their full potential. Far too often, self-doubt and fear of failure prevent us from taking that leap of faith and embracing our greatness. But what if, just for a moment, we set aside our doubts and allowed ourselves to truly explore our strengths, talents, and unique abilities? What if we dared to think outside of the box and invested in our belief in ourselves? The results could be nothing short of extraordinary.

Each one of us possesses an incredible reservoir of untapped potential. However, it is only by giving ourselves a chance that we can unlock this hidden greatness. It begins with a journey inward, a sincere examination of our strengths and talents. By identifying and developing these strong points, we lay the foundation for our success.

Think of yourself as a diamond in the rough. You have the potential to shine brilliantly, but it requires effort, patience, and a willingness to invest in self-improvement. Take the time to discover what truly brings you joy and fulfillment. Nurture those passions and talents, for they are the keys to unlocking your greatness.

It is also crucial to break free from the confines of conventional thinking. The world is changing rapidly, and the most successful individuals are those who can adapt and think outside of the box.

Embrace innovation, challenge the status quo, and be unafraid to take calculated risks. By doing so, you open up a world of possibilities and pave the way for greatness to flow into your life.

However, none of this is possible without a strong belief in oneself. Confidence is the driving force behind every successful person. Believe in your abilities, your dreams, and your potential. Surround yourself with positive influences, seek out mentors who can guide you, and never underestimate the power of self-affirmation.

It is important to recognize that greatness does not come easily or overnight. It is a journey, filled with obstacles and setbacks. But it is through these challenges that we grow, learn, and become stronger. Embrace failure as a stepping stone to success and never let setbacks deter you from pursuing your dreams.

So, I implore you to give yourself a chance. Look deep within, develop your strong points, and allow yourself the opportunity to think outside of the box. Invest in and strengthen your belief in yourself. Know that you have what it takes to be great. Believe it, embrace it, and watch as your greatness flows effortlessly into every aspect of your life.

LISBON

Photos: Katherine Maher, CEO, Web Summit, on Q&A stage during day two of Web Summit 2023 at the Altice Arena in Lisbon, Portugal. Photo by Harry Murphy/Web Summit via Sportsfile) #websummit #Lisbon #KatherineMaher #vmhmagazine #innovators #tech

"I feel a huge responsibility, it (Web Summit) is a community of people who care very deeply about Web Summit," said Katherine Maher the new CEO of Web Summit

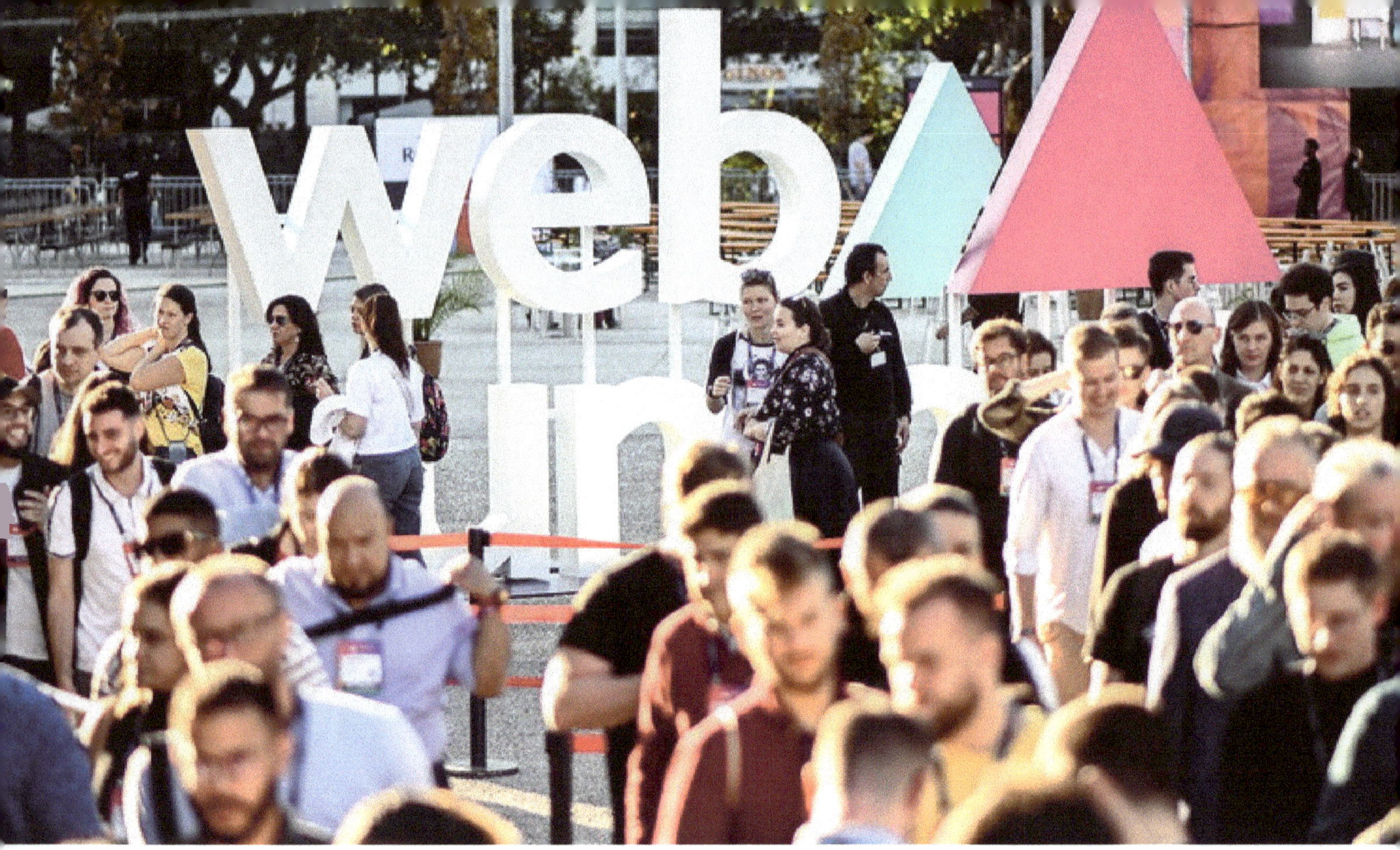

"We've brought together tens of thousands of people who have used this week in Lisbon as a springboard to do remarkable things," said Katherine Maher, the new CEO of Web Summit. The event allows innovators "to launch companies, find investors, unveil projects, and advance a vision of the world worth debating".

"I feel a huge responsibility, it (Web Summit) is a community of people who care very deeply about Web Summit," said Katherine Maher the new CEO of Web Summit. With these words, Maher encapsulates the essence of this extraordinary event that has become a catalyst for innovation, collaboration, and positive change.

Taking over from former CEO Paddy Cosgrave, Maher steps into her role with a deep understanding of the responsibility she holds. The Web Summit is not just a conference; it is a vibrant community of individuals who are passionate about leveraging technology to transform the world. Maher recognizes the importance of nurturing this community and providing them with the tools and opportunities they need to thrive.

(

websummit

Embracing Authenticity: Reclaiming Your True Identity

Written by
Vikki Jones

Have you ever felt like you've lost touch with who you really are? Maybe you've been going through the motions, conforming to societal expectations, and suppressing your true self. Well, it's time to reclaim your identity!

Reclaiming your identity means rediscovering and reconnecting with the unique qualities that make you who you are. It's about understanding your values, passions, and interests, and embracing them wholeheartedly. In this journey of self-discovery, you'll find a renewed sense of authenticity, confidence, and fulfillment. So, let's delve into what it truly means to reclaim your identity and embark on a path of self-acceptance and personal growth.

In a world that often pressures us to conform, it's not uncommon to lose sight of our true selves. However, it's time to break free from these molds and embrace our authentic identities. Reclaiming who we truly are is a powerful journey of self-discovery and self-acceptance, allowing us to live a more fulfilling and meaningful life. Let's delve deeper into the significance of authenticity and explore a few key pointers that can help us reclaim our true identities.

1. Self-Reflection:

To reclaim our identity, it is vital to engage in self-reflection. Take a moment to pause, disconnect from external influences, and understanding these core aspects of yourself, you can align your actions and choices with your true identity.

2. Letting Go of Expectations:

Society often imposes expectations and standards upon us, dictating how we should look, behave, or succeed. These societal pressures can hinder our ability to embrace our authentic selves. Reclaiming your identity means liberating yourself from these external pressures and allowing your true self to shine. Embrace the freedom of being unapologetically you, without seeking validation or conforming to others' expectations.

3. Honoring Your Passions:

Rediscovering your true identity involves reigniting your passions. Reflect on the activities, hobbies, or interests that bring you immense joy and fulfillment. These are often the areas where your authentic self thrives. Allow yourself the time and space to engage in these activities regularly. Whether it's art, music, writing, or any other creative outlet, pursuing your passions will help you reconnect with your true identity and bring a sense of purpose and fulfillment to your life.

4. Surrounding Yourself with Authenticity:

Creating a supportive environment is crucial in reclaiming your identity. Surround yourself with people who appreciate and support your true self. Authentic relationships and connections can provide a nurturing space for personal growth. Seek out individuals who celebrate your uniqueness, embrace your quirks, and encourage you to stay true to yourself. By being around authentic individuals, you will feel more comfortable and confident in expressing your true identity.

Reclaiming your identity is a transformative journey that requires self-reflection, letting go of expectations, honoring your passions, and surrounding yourself with authenticity. Embracing your true self is a powerful act of self-love and acceptance, allowing you to live a life that aligns with your values and brings you genuine happiness. So, let's embark on this journey together, embracing authenticity and reclaiming our true identities. Remember, you are unique, valuable, and worthy of being authentically you.

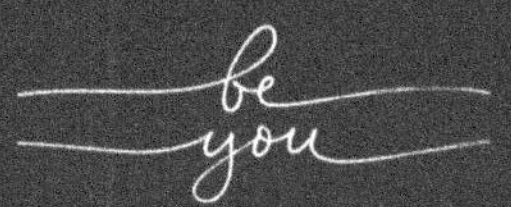

'Losing oneself can happen for various reasons, and it can be an unsettling and disorienting experience. It often involves feelings of confusion, detachment, and a lack of purpose. However, recognizing that you have lost yourself is an important first step towards reclaiming your true identity. Take the time to reflect on who you were before and compare it to who you are now. Identify the aspects of yourself that have changed or been overshadowed, and pinpoint the factors that contributed to this loss. Acknowledging these differences can provide clarity and motivation to make the necessary adjustments towards rediscovering your authentic self.

Once you have recognized the changes and understood the reasons behind losing yourself, it becomes essential to reclaim your true identity. Start by reconnecting with the activities, hobbies, and interests that used to bring you joy and fulfillment. By revisiting these passions, you can tap into the core of who you are and start rebuilding your sense of self. Additionally, take the time for self-reflection and introspection. Explore your values, beliefs, and personal goals to gain a clearer understanding of who you truly are and where you want to go. Surround yourself with supportive individuals who appreciate and accept you for who you are, as they can provide encouragement and assistance along your journey of self-reclamation. Remember, reclaiming yourself is a process that requires patience, self-compassion, and a commitment to personal growth. By embracing this journey, you can regain your sense of identity and live a more fulfilled and authentic life.'

PERSONAL GROWTH & SUCCESS
UNLOCKING YOUR GREATEST POTENTIAL

Life is a journey of constant growth and self-discovery. Often, we find ourselves in a state of complacency, unaware that there is a greater place waiting for us. It is during these uncomfortable moments that we have the opportunity to develop our character, enhance our skills, and prepare ourselves for the next level. Embracing discomfort becomes the key to unlocking our greatest potential. In this editorial, we will explore the importance of pushing through, focusing, and challenging ourselves to reach new heights in life.

1. The Comfort Zone Illusion:

The comfort zone is a deceptive place, where we may feel safe and secure, but it hinders our personal growth. It is in the discomfort that we truly learn and evolve as individuals. Stepping out of our comfort zone allows us to expand our horizons, face new challenges, and discover hidden talents. Embracing discomfort is the first step towards breaking free from the limitations we set for ourselves.

2. Character Development:

When faced with discomfort, we are forced to confront our fears and insecurities. This process builds resilience, determination, and character. Overcoming obstacles strengthens our mental and emotional muscles, enabling us to handle future challenges with greater ease. Embracing discomfort becomes an opportunity for personal growth and self-improvement, shaping us into stronger and more capable individuals.

3. Skill Enhancement:

In the pursuit of our greatest place, we must continuously refine and develop our skills. Embracing discomfort pushes us to acquire new knowledge, learn from our mistakes, and adapt to unfamiliar situations. It is through these experiences that we acquire the expertise and abilities necessary to excel in our chosen fields. Each moment of discomfort becomes an opportunity to sharpen our skills and become better versions of ourselves.

4. Preparation for the Next Level:

Life is a series of stepping stones, and each discomfort we encounter prepares us for the next level. By embracing discomfort, we become better equipped to handle the challenges that lie ahead. Our ability to adapt, persevere, and thrive in uncomfortable situations becomes a valuable asset as we progress towards our goals.

Embracing discomfort is not only about reaching our greatest place but also about preparing ourselves for the journey that follows.

5. Determination and Intentionality:

To embrace discomfort, we must approach it with determination and intentionality. It is not enough to simply endure discomfort; we must actively seek out opportunities for growth and self-improvement. This requires setting clear goals, breaking them down into manageable steps, and committing ourselves to the process.

With a focused mindset and unwavering determination, we can navigate through discomfort and emerge stronger on the other side.

Embracing discomfort is a necessary step in our journey towards self-actualization. It is through these uncomfortable moments that we learn, grow, and prepare ourselves for our greatest place in life. By stepping out of our comfort zone, we develop our character, enhance our skills, and become better equipped to face the challenges that lie ahead. Let us embrace discomfort with determination and intentionality, knowing that our greatest potential awaits us on the other side.

COMFORTABLE CARRYING OPTIONS

Say goodbye to uncomfortable bags. Vikki Jones' designs prioritize comfort, with padded straps, ergonomic handles, and lightweight construction, ensuring a comfortable carrying experience even during long journeys.

Need extra space? Jones' bags feature expandable compartments, allowing you to increase the capacity when needed. Travel with confidence, knowing you have room for souvenirs or extra work documents.

The Power of SMEs: Adapting to Global Solutions

By Vikki Jones

Small and Medium-sized Enterprises (SMEs) play a vital role in the global economy, driving innovation, job creation, and economic growth. However, in times of disruption and uncertainty, such as the recent COVID-19 pandemic, these enterprises often face immense challenges that can threaten their survival. It is crucial to recognize the importance of supporting and strengthening SMEs, particularly when it comes to building resilient supply chains.

Building a resilient supply chain within SMEs is a critical aspect that deserves attention. SMEs often find themselves vulnerable to disruptions caused by various factors, including economic downturns, natural disasters, trade restrictions, and logistical challenges. These disruptions can have far-reaching consequences, impacting not only the SMEs themselves but also the larger economy.

Therefore, it is paramount to enhance the resilience of SMEs and their supply chains. This can be achieved through proactive measures and strategic planning. Governments, policymakers, and industry leaders must come together to develop supportive policies, establish risk management frameworks, and foster collaborations between SMEs and larger enterprises. By doing so, we can create an environment that enables SMEs to thrive, even in the face of adversity.

One crucial aspect of building resilient supply chains for SMEs is diversification. Relying on a single supplier or market can expose SMEs to substantial risks if disruption occurs. Encouraging SMEs to diversify their suppliers and customer bases can help mitigate these risks and ensure a more robust supply chain. By expanding their networks and exploring new markets, SMEs can decrease their dependence on a single source of revenue, enhancing their ability to adapt to changing circumstances.

Moreover, leveraging technology and digital solutions can significantly enhance both the efficiency and resilience of SMEs. Embracing e-commerce platforms, cloud-based systems, and digital communication tools can enable SMEs to streamline operations, access new markets, and expand their reach.

Technology can also facilitate real-time data tracking, allowing SMEs to identify vulnerabilities in their supply chains and take proactive measures to address them swiftly. Implementing innovative technologies provides SMEs with the agility necessary to navigate disruptions and maintain their competitiveness in the global market.

Relying on a single supplier or market ca[n] expose SMEs to substantial risks if disruption occurs.

Another crucial aspect to consider is access to finance. SMEs often face constraints when seeking funding to invest in technology, expand their operations, or withstand economic shocks. Governments and financial institutions need to provide tailored financial services and support mechanisms specifically designed for SMEs. Implementing programs that offer flexible financing options, grants, and business development services can empower SMEs to invest in their growth and resilience.

Prioritizing the resilience of SMEs and building robust supply chains is of utmost importance for economic stability and growth. By adopting proactive measures such as diversification, leveraging technology, and ensuring access to finance, we can safeguard the sustainability of SMEs and strengthen their contributions to the economy. Collaboration between governments, policymakers, industry leaders, and SMEs themselves will be pivotal in creating an environment that fosters resilience and empowers the backbone of our economy. With the right support, SMEs can effectively adapt to global solutions, driving forward progress and overcoming challenges presented by an ever-changing world.creating an environment that fosters resilience and empowers them further.

Key Tips for Enhancing SMEs and Building Strong Supply Chains

1. Diversify Suppliers and Customer Bases: Encourage SMEs to expand their networks and explore new markets to reduce reliance on a single supplier or customer. By diversifying, SMEs can mitigate risks and build a more robust supply chain that can adapt to changing circumstances.

2. Embrace Technology and Digital Solutions: SMEs should leverage e-commerce platforms, cloud-based systems, and digital communication tools to streamline operations, access new markets, and enhance efficiency. Implementing innovative technologies enables SMEs to stay agile and competitive in the global market.

3. Focus on Risk Management and Planning: Governments, policymakers, and industry leaders must collaborate to develop supportive policies and risk management frameworks. Proactive planning ensures SMEs have the necessary tools to anticipate and navigate disruptions effectively.

4. Ensure Access to Finance: Tailored financial services and support mechanisms should be provided by governments and financial institutions. Flexible financing options, grants, and business development services empower SMEs to invest in their growth and resilience, strengthening their contributions to the economy.

5. Foster Collaborative Relationships: Encourage collaboration between SMEs and larger enterprises to share resources, knowledge, and expertise. Such partnerships can lead to innovative solutions, foster resilience, and create an environment where SMEs can thrive even in challenging times.

By following these key tips, SMEs can enhance their ability to adapt, build resilient supply chains, and continue driving innovation, job creation, and economic growth in the global economy.

the resilience of the human spirit

"Overcoming Trauma" is a testament to the power of personal storytelling and the transformative nature of resilience.

OVERCOMING TRAUMA

WRITTEN BY

VIKKI HANKINS

Product Details:
ISBN-13: 9798985334968
Publisher: VMH Publishing
Publication date: 11/16/2023
Pages: 552
Product Weight: 1.4 lbs.
Product Dimensions: 5.50(w) x 8.50(h) x 1.23(d)

AVAILABLE IN-STORE AT:

BOOKS Kinokuniya
123 ASTRONAUT E. S.
ONIZUKA ST, #205
LOS ANGELES, CA
90012

"Overcoming Trauma" is a testament to the resilience of the human spirit. Vikki Hankins' honest and introspective memoir serves as a beacon of hope for those who have experienced their own traumas, showing that it is possible to rise above the darkest moments and reclaim one's life. Her powerful story reminds us that through self-reflection, acceptance, and the courage to confront our pain, we can find the strength to heal and truly live again. "Overcoming Trauma" is a testament to the power of personal storytelling and the transformative nature of resilience.

ALSO AVAILABLE ONLINE AT:

amazon.com BARNES&NOBLE BOOKSELLERS
Walmart TARGET

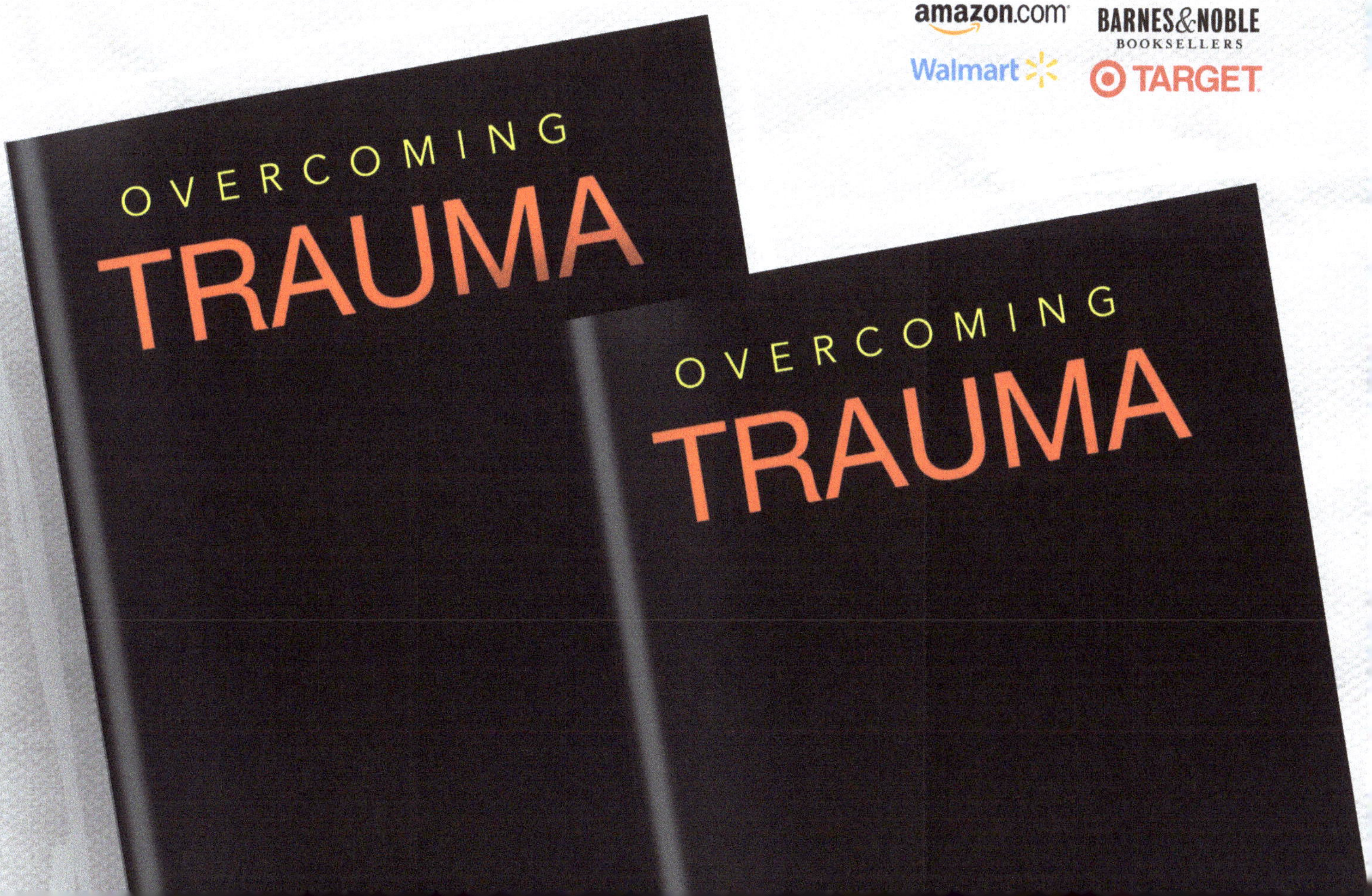

EMBRACING COURAGE TO CONQUER TRAUMA

In a world where trauma often leaves deep scars, recognizing the transformative potential of courage involves facing our pain and releasing what no longer serves us. However, it is important to be mindful that healing is a process and not a 'one-size-fits-all' solution.

In the depths of trauma, it is the unwavering courage of the human spirit that propels individuals forward, enabling them to conquer the most formidable challenges. Vikki Hankins' memoir, "<u>Overcoming Trauma</u>," serves as a powerful testament to the indomitable resilience of the human spirit and the transformative power of facing one's trauma head-on.

Hankins' memoir is a profound and introspective account of her personal journey through the darkest corridors of trauma. With unflinching honesty, she lays bare the depths of her pain, providing a raw glimpse into the immense struggle that trauma inflicts upon the human psyche. However, it is her unwavering courage and determination to confront her past that truly captivates readers.

"<u>Overcoming Trauma</u>" highlights the immense bravery required to face one's trauma, as it is through this courageous act that true healing can begin. Hankins emphasizes the importance of self-reflection, urging individuals to delve into the depths of their pain and confront the demons that haunt them. It is through this process of fearless introspection that the seeds of healing are sown.

The journey towards healing and recovery is by no means an easy one. It demands immense courage to confront the wounds of the past, to relive the pain, and to acknowledge the vulnerabilities that trauma has left in its wake. Yet, it is precisely this courage that paves the way for transformation and growth.

Hankins' memoir serves as a beacon of hope, reminding us that the human spirit possesses an unwavering resilience that can triumph over even the most profound trauma. By sharing her own story, she not only finds solace and healing but also inspires others to embark on their own path towards recovery. Through her words, she creates a sense of unity, assuring readers that they are not alone in their struggles.

The courage to confront trauma not only aids in healing but also serves as a catalyst for personal growth. It is through the courageous act of facing our pain that we can begin to rebuild our lives, reclaim our identities, and find newfound strength within ourselves. The transformative power of this courage cannot be understated, as it allows individuals to move beyond their trauma and embrace a future filled with hope and possibility.

In a world where trauma often leaves individuals feeling shattered and broken, it is crucial to recognize and celebrate the courage it takes to face it head-on. We must amplify the stories of resilience and bravery, for they serve as a reminder that healing is possible, even in the face of unimaginable pain. "Overcoming Trauma" stands as a testament to the triumph of the human spirit, urging us all to harness our courage and support one another in our collective journey towards healing.

Ultimately, it is through the unwavering courage to confront trauma that the human spirit finds its greatest strength. By embracing this courage, we can unlock the transformative power within us, transcending our past and forging a future defined by resilience, growth, and the unwavering spirit of triumph.

5 Tips to Manage Money Smarter

There's more to managing your money than paying your bills and successfully avoiding overdraft charges (although those are definitely steps in the right direction). Effectively managing your money takes time and planning, but the payoff may be a stronger financial future.

Create a budget. Some people avoid making a monthly budget because they think they don't need one. However, having a clear idea of the money coming in and going out of your bank account each month can help you make better spending decisions. A budget doesn't have to be complicated; it can be as simple as a spreadsheet that lists your monthly income and expenses. Be sure to consider long-term debt, like student loans, and treat your savings account as a payee you owe each month.

Track your spending. In a similar vein, it's a good idea to see where your non-bill-related spending goes. For example, you may stop by the grocery store more frequently than you realize, and each of those trips is likely going to cost you more than if you limited it to just once or twice a week. Many banks and credit institutions offer charts and graphs that break down your spending so you can see exactly where your money is going and use that information to make adjustments.

Research big purchases. What constitutes "big" may vary depending on your circumstances and financial status, but regardless of the dollar amount, doing some due diligence before purchases is a good idea. The average millennial will do 4.6 hours of research before buying a big-ticket item like a mattress or car, according to a survey conducted by OnePoll on behalf of Mattress Firm.

Millennials are also likely to seek input from others, with one in five consulting four or more people for their opinions on a purchase.

"Doing research before making a big purchase can make all the difference," said Timothy Mayes, Mattress Firm's senior manager of eCommerce merchandising. "There are several resources available such as online reviews, blogs and even guides on the best time to buy that can help save you money on larger purchases. If you find yourself overwhelmed with too many options, recommendations from friends and family are the best resources to help you narrow down your choices."

Prepare for emergencies. If a single unexpected event would cripple you financially, it's a good idea to build an emergency fund that could help you weather through a storm. A job loss, accident or illness would substantially alter your income, expenses or both, so having at least a few months of salary stashed in savings could make a major difference in how long that unfortunate scenario affects your life.

Finance purchases responsibly. Building credit takes time and responsibility, but if you don't ever borrow money, you won't have a chance to earn the rates reserved for exceptional credit holders. Financing a moderately sized purchase, such as a mattress, is a good starting point. It may be out of reach for a cash payment, but the balance you carry could be paid in a reasonably short timeframe. To build good credit, always make payments on time and make monthly payments larger than the minimum payment – which is usually just the interest – so you're actually paying down the principal. Following these tips and taking advantage of product sites that offer resources and information on a potential purchase may aid in your long-term financial health. Find more information at MattressFirm.com/blog.

IGNITING LUXURY & SUSTAINABILITY

THE LAUNCH OF **MENA 360° PRIVATE CLUB**, SHOWCASING SUCCESS AND GO GREEN INITIATIVES AT THE **HABTOOR PALACE, DUBAI**

WRITTEN BY VIKKI JONES

In a night filled with glamour and exclusivity, the grand opening of MENA 360° Private Club at Habtoor Palace in Dubai left no stone unturned in promising an extravagant gala that would captivate the elite. This invitation-only affair brought together 200 select guests, including renowned celebrities from the world of film, sports, and entertainment. The event offered an exceptional opportunity for these esteemed individuals to become part of an exclusive private club and indulge in a world of luxury and success.

Headquartered in Dubai, MENA 360° reigns as a vibrant entity that has carved its name in international investments, eco-conscious solutions, event intellectual properties, marketing, public relations, and business strategies. Established by industry heavyweights Liza Amani, Garen Mehrabian, Maximilian Reidl, and Ramin Seyed, this partnership has created a unique business hub in the region, showcasing groundbreaking projects and innovative ideas that have the potential to revolutionize various industries.

The grand evening commenced with a gala dinner, drawing high-profile personalities from around the world.This exceptional gathering offered guests an exclusive opportunity to connect with industry giants, political leaders, and successful entrepreneurs.

HABTOOR PALACE INTERIOR (PHOTO CREDIT: FARAH BOOTWALA)

Through these interactions, valuable networks were forged, fostering collaborations that hold the potential to shape the future.

The event took place at The Habtoor Palace, an epitome of elegance and luxury. Nestled on the banks of the Dubai Water Canal, this luxurious establishment is designed to transport guests into a world of opulence. The sprawling gardens, three sparkling pools, and fine dining options further added to the allure of this grand venue. However, what truly set The Habtoor Palace apart were its world-class amenities, particularly its signature suites that offered an unparalleled experience.

HABTOOR PALACE INTERIOR (PHOTO CREDIT: FARAH BOOTWALA)

HABTOOR PALACE INTERIOR (PHOTO CREDIT: FARAH BOOTWALA)

One of the highlights of the evening was the breathtaking fashion showcase by Turkish designer Ebru Berkiden. Berkiden expressed her profound honor in showcasing her modern abaya collection on such a magnificent stage. She drew inspiration from the vibrant culture and heritage of the nation, which resonated deeply with her designs. Berkiden extended her heartfelt gratitude to Mr. Ramin Seyed and his team for granting her the opportunity to participate in a historical event. "I am profoundly honored to have showcased my fashion line on such a magnificent stage in the UAE...Following the show's success, I've received attention from internationally acclaimed fashion institutions and invitations to prominent Middle Eastern fashion events which I look forward to attend," said Berkiden.

During the event, attention was also drawn to the visionary sustainable project, GO GREEN. MENA 360° co-founder Garen Mehrabian highlighted the powerful message conveyed by former H.E. Dr. Mohammed S. Al Kindi. Dr. Al Kindi, the former Minister for Environment & Water in the UAE's Cabinet, emphasized the urgent need to forge a sustainable future for coming generations. With this in mind, Mehrabian emphasized that he was not just an activist but a forward-thinking, conscious businessman who firmly believed in green and innovative solutions.

Mehrabian pointed out the irony of discussing sustainability while incurring a significant environmental cost by gathering people from over 11 countries. However, he announced a partnership with the GRO Foundation *(grofoundation.io/mena-360/)* to address this issue. Quoting Mehrabian directly, he said, "The event's carbon footprint was calculated at 564.61 tons. To offset this, we need to plant 20,622 trees. However, GoGreen.World, in collaboration with the GRO Foundation, has already planted 100,000 trees, not just offsetting our impact but contributing positively to the environment."

Furthermore, Mehrabian revealed a game-changing product, ENKI, which saves over 60% of water usage and boosts 30% more harvest without the need for fertilizers or chemicals. Quoting Mehrabian again, he stated, "This underscores our commitment to eco-friendly solutions, encouraging all 220 attendees to join us on this journey. Every product, every choice we make is a step towards a brighter, thriving world. Let's unite under GoGreen.world to ignite significant changes, creating a legacy of sustainability and hope."

GAREN MEHRABIAN PHOTO CREDIT: RUBEN DANIELYAN

GAREN MEHRABIAN PHOTO CREDIT: RUBEN DANIELYAN

"This underscores our commitment to eco-friendly solutions, encouraging all 220 attendees to join us on this journey. Every product, every choice we make is a step towards a brighter, thriving world..."

The grand opening of MENA 360° Private Club at Habtoor Palace was more than just an exclusive event; it was a glimpse into a world where luxury and success coalesced. As industry giants, political leaders, and celebrities came together under one roof, it became clear that this club offered much more than opulence. It embodied a culture of collaboration, innovation, and sustainability, paving the way for a brighter future.

Looking ahead, MENA 360° plans to host additional events in the future. These events, structured as yearly gatherings, will maintain their invite-only status to ensure a curated and bespoke experience for attendees. This format allows for a more focused and impactful engagement among participants, often drawing in a select group of influencers, industry leaders, and key decision-makers from various sectors. The exclusivity of these events has become a hallmark of MENA 360°, providing a unique platform for networking, collaboration, and the exchange of ideas within the Middle East and North African region.

LAUNCH OF MENA 360° PRIVATE CLUB

LIZA AMANI & ANNA OSERSKA PHOTO CREDIT: RUBEN DANIELYAN

RAMIN SEYED & EBRU BERKIDEN PHOTO CREDIT: RUBEN DANIELYAN

PHOTO CREDIT: RUBEN DANIELYAN

AHLLAM, PHOTO CREDIT: RUBEN DANIELYAN

UNLOCK YOUR POWER WITHIN

FACETS OF THE HEART TRANSFORMATION FROM THE INSIDE OUT

- Tap into your inner strength and courage to embrace positive change.
- Dontisha James shares her insights gained from captivating speaking engagements.
- Gain profound knowledge and practical tools to unlock your full potential.
- Embrace the powerful role of faith and spirituality in achieving true transformation.
- Understand the impact of personal transformation on society as a whole.

PURCHASE NOW

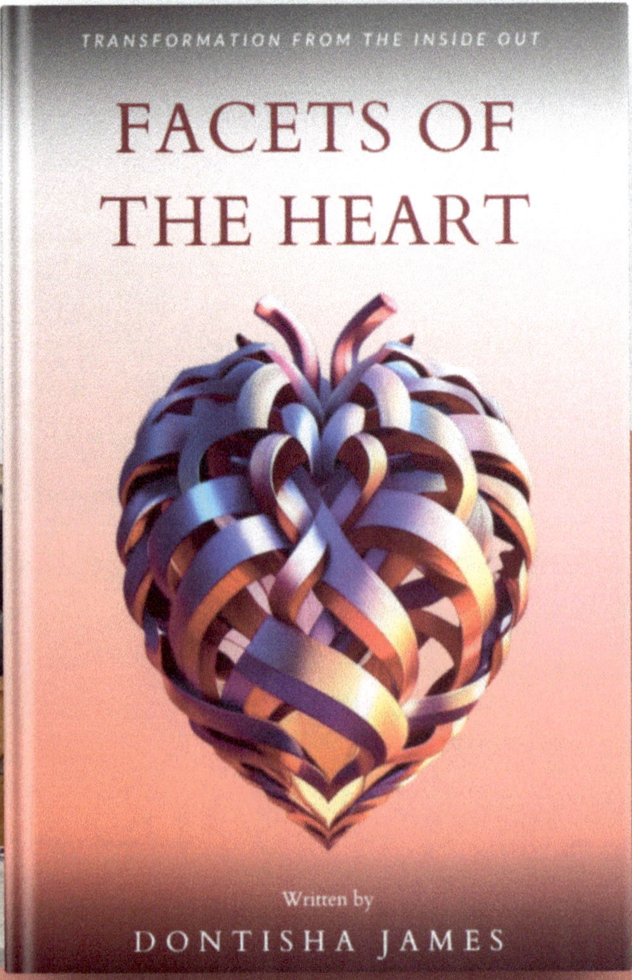

Written by Vikki Jones

BOOSTING SMALL AND MEDIUM-SIZED BUSINESSES:

HOW AI AND CHATGPT CAN HELP

Have you ever wondered how big companies always seem to have the upper hand when it comes to new technologies like Artificial Intelligence (AI)? It's because they have the money and staff to quickly jump on the AI bandwagon and make the most of it, while small and medium-sized businesses (SMEs) struggle to keep up. But shouldn't there be a way for smaller companies to increase their profits and tap into the full potential of AI too?

Well, the good news is that there is hope for SMEs to level the playing field and benefit from AI and the recently released ChatGPT. These fancy tech tools have a lot to offer, but it's understandable that smaller businesses might be hesitant to trust and adopt them. After all, they don't have an army of tech experts at their disposal like the big guys do.

But fear not, because there are practical ways for SMEs to embrace AI and ChatGPT without breaking the bank or feeling overwhelmed. The first step is education and awareness. SMEs need to take the time to learn about the benefits and possibilities that AI and ChatGPT can bring to their operations.

By understanding how these technologies can improve efficiency and productivity in specific areas, SMEs can start reaping the rewards.

Building trust is another crucial factor. AI might seem like a scary and unpredictable thing, but SMEs can ease their worries by partnering with reliable AI providers and starting with small-scale pilot projects. Seeing tangible results and success stories within their own industry will help SMEs gain confidence in AI as a valuable tool for their business.

Collaboration is key too. SMEs can team up with other small businesses or even larger companies to share resources, expertise, and navigate the AI landscape together. By working together, they can overcome the lack of technical talent and benefit from collective knowledge, which will ultimately level the playing field against their bigger competitors.

It's also important for governments and industry associations to lend a helping hand. They can offer incentives, grants, and specialized programs to support SMEs in implementing AI technologies. By creating an environment that promotes knowledge-sharing, collaboration, and innovation, policymakers can empower SMEs to fully embrace AI and unlock its potential.

Yes, the challenges of adopting AI and ChatGPT might seem challenging for SMEs, but it's important to remember that every new technology brings opportunities for growth and success. By seeking knowledge, building trust, embracing collaboration, and taking advantage of supportive policies, small and medium-sized businesses can harness the power of AI and ChatGPT to increase their profits, work more efficiently, and thrive in a competitive market.

PRACTICAL WAYS
SME'S CAN UTILIZE AI

Small and medium-sized enterprises (SMEs) can leverage the power of Artificial Intelligence (AI) in various ways to enhance their operations, improve efficiency, and drive growth.

1. **Customer Service and Support:** AI-powered chatbots and virtual assistants can handle customer inquiries, provide real-time support, and offer personalized recommendations. These AI-driven solutions can streamline customer interactions, reduce response times, and improve customer satisfaction, even outside regular business hours.

2. **Data Analysis and Insights:** AI algorithms can process large volumes of data quickly and accurately, enabling SMEs to gain valuable insights. By analyzing customer behavior, market trends, and operational data, SMEs can make informed decisions, identify patterns, and predict future trends. This helps in optimizing marketing strategies, inventory management, and overall business operations.

3. **Predictive Maintenance:** AI can help SMEs implement predictive maintenance strategies by analyzing data from sensors and machines. By detecting patterns and anomalies, AI algorithms can predict equipment failures or maintenance needs, allowing SMEs to proactively address issues before they escalate. This minimizes downtime, reduces maintenance costs, and extends the lifespan of machinery and assets.

4. **Process Automation:** AI-powered automation can streamline repetitive and time-consuming tasks, freeing up employees to focus on more strategic and value-added activities. SMEs can use AI to automate data entry, invoice processing, inventory management, and other routine tasks, improving operational efficiency and reducing errors.

5. **Sales and Marketing Optimization:** AI can enhance SMEs' sales and marketing efforts by analyzing customer data, identifying leads, and personalizing marketing campaigns. AI algorithms can segment customers based on their preferences, purchase history, and behavior, enabling SMEs to deliver targeted and relevant marketing messages. This helps in boosting conversion rates, increasing customer engagement, and optimizing sales funnels.

6. **Personalized Customer Experiences:** AI enables SMEs to deliver personalized experiences by analyzing customer preferences, behavior, and past interactions. AI algorithms can recommend products, content, and services tailored to each customer's specific needs and interests. This enhances customer satisfaction, loyalty, and drives repeat business.

7. **Market Research and Competitive Analysis:** SMEs can leverage AI to gather and analyze market data, customer reviews, social media sentiment, and competitor information. AI-powered tools can provide valuable insights into market trends, consumer preferences, and competitive intelligence. This helps SMEs make data-driven decisions, identify market gaps, and develop competitive strategies.

8. **Virtual Collaboration and Communication:** With the rise of remote work, AI-powered virtual collaboration tools can facilitate communication, project management, and knowledge sharing among remote teams. AI-driven solutions can automate scheduling, generate meeting summaries, and provide real-time language translation, enabling SMEs to collaborate effectively across borders and time zones.

VIKKI JONES

DESIGNER

COMFORTABLE
CARRYING OPTIONS

Say goodbye to uncomfortable bags. Vikki Jones' designs prioritize comfort, with padded straps, ergonomic handles, and lightweight construction, ensuring a comfortable carrying experience even during long journeys.

Need extra space? Jones' bags feature expandable compartments, allowing you to increase the capacity when needed. Travel with confidence, knowing you have room for souvenirs or extra work documents.

LUXURY
CREATIONS
VIKKIJONES.COM

Reinventing Yourself: Embracing Vitality in All Areas of Life for Maximum Benefits

The concept of reinventing oneself has become more important than ever. Embracing vitality in all aspects of life not only ensures personal growth and fulfillment but also positively impacts one's profession. By incorporating new things into our professional lives, we open doors to fresh opportunities, increased productivity, and overall success. This article explores the significance of reinventing oneself and how it benefits all aspects of life, including professional growth.

1. Unleashing Personal Growth:

Reinventing oneself is a transformative process that encourages personal growth in all areas of life. By embracing vitality, we challenge ourselves to step out of our comfort zones, explore new interests, and adopt a growth mindset. This not only enhances our skills and knowledge but also broadens our perspectives, making us more adaptable and resilient. As we reinvent ourselves, we become more confident, self-aware, and open to new experiences, ultimately leading to a more fulfilling life.

2. Achieving Balance and Wellness:

Vitality is not limited to professional success alone; it extends to all aspects of life, including physical, mental, and emotional well-being. Reinventing ourselves allows us to prioritize self-care, maintain a healthy work-life balance, and cultivate overall wellness. By incorporating new habits, such as exercise, meditation, or pursuing hobbies, we create a harmonious equilibrium that positively impacts our personal and professional lives. A balanced individual is more likely to excel in their career, build meaningful relationships, and experience greater satisfaction in life.

3. Boosting Professional Growth:

Reinventing oneself in professional settings is a powerful tool for career advancement and success. By incorporating new things into our profession, such as learning new skills, embracing emerging technologies, or pursuing additional education, we position ourselves at the forefront of our industry. This continuous growth not only enhances our expertise but

Embracing a Growth Mindset: Reinventing oneself is closely linked to adopting a growth mindset.

also makes us more adaptable to changing market demands. Additionally, reinventing ourselves professionally opens doors to new opportunities, expands our network, and increases our chances of career progression.

4. Fostering Creativity and Innovation: Reinvention encourages creativity and innovation, both of which are vital in today's competitive world. By embracing new ideas, exploring different perspectives, and incorporating fresh approaches, we unlock our creative potential. This not only benefits our personal lives by sparking joy and fulfillment but also contributes to our professional success. A creative and innovative professional is more likely to find unique solutions to challenges, think outside the box, and stand out among their peers.

5. Stepping Out of Comfort Zones: Reinvention often requires stepping out of our comfort zones and embracing new experiences. Whether it's learning a new skill, pursuing a different career path, or exploring a new hobby, these unfamiliar territories push us to grow and adapt. By challenging ourselves and taking calculated risks, we develop resilience, confidence, and a broader perspective on life.

6. Discovering New Passions and Purpose: Through the process of reinvention, we have the opportunity to explore new interests, passions, and purposes.

By stepping out of our comfort zones and trying new things, we may stumble upon hidden talents or discover activities that bring us joy and fulfillment. This exploration helps us align our lives with our true passions and purpose, leading to a more meaningful and fulfilling existence.

7. Self-Reflection and Awareness: When we decide to reinvent ourselves, we embark on a journey of self-reflection and self-awareness. We question our beliefs, values, and behaviors, and assess if they align with our true desires and aspirations. This introspection helps us gain a deeper understanding of ourselves and identify areas where personal growth is needed.

Reinventing oneself leads to personal growth by fostering self-reflection, pushing us out of our comfort zones, embracing a growth mindset, expanding knowledge and skills, building resilience and adaptability, and discovering new passions and purpose. It is through this transformative process that we can unlock our full potential and lead a more fulfilling lives.